The Boston Globe

This magazine is available in quantity at special discounts for your group or organization.
For further information, contact:

Triumph Books LLC
814 North Franklin Street
Chicago, Illinois 60610
Phone: (312) 337-0747
www.triumphbooks.com

Printed in U.S.A.
ISBN: 978-1-60078-985-4

TRIUMPH
BOOKS

TRIUMPHBOOKS**.COM**

ART DIRECTOR Ryan Huddle
EDITOR Janice Page
ASSISTANT EDITOR/WRITER Ron Driscoll
PHOTOGRAPHERS (Globe staff) Yoon S. Byun, Barry Chin, Jim Davis, Darren Durlach, Bill Greene, Pat Greenhouse, Stan Grossfeld, Suzanne Kreiter, and John Tlumacki; (for the Globe) Jessica Rinaldi

With special thanks to Boston Globe publisher Christopher Mayer and editor Brian McGrory; Joe Sullivan, Luke Knox, and the Boston Globe sports department; Bill Greene and the Globe photo department; Lisa Tuite and the Globe library staff; Globe executive director of communications Ellen Clegg; Mary Zanor, John Gates, and Elevate Communications; Mitch Rogatz, Kristine Anstrats, and everyone at Triumph Books; Chris Jackson and Quad/Graphics of Taunton; Todd Shuster, Lane Zachary, and Zachary Shuster Harmsworth Literary Agency.

Cover photo: World Series MVP David Ortiz celebrated as the duck boats rumbled out of Fenway Park.
Previous pages: Ortiz enjoyed every mile of the rolling rally, and Red Sox right fielder Shane Victorino displayed the spoils of victory on Tremont Street.

Contents

A CELEBRATION OF THE WORLD CHAMPION 2013 BOSTON RED SOX

6 — **Introduction**
by Red Sox manager John Farrell.

8 — **Redeem Team**
The Red Sox completed a remarkable turnaround, proving that chemistry can trump talent. By Christopher L. Gasper.

10 — **It All Worked**
Boston's Bearded Brotherhood is a classic example of the whole being greater than the parts. By Dan Shaughnessy.

20 — **World Series**
The Red Sox vanquished the Cardinals in six games, riding the bat of MVP David Ortiz, strong pitching from Jon Lester and John Lackey, and a few timely hits to their third duck-boat parade in a decade.

66 — **ALCS**
The Tigers' vaunted starters tested Boston, but the Sox rallied to win Game 2, got their own strong outings from John Lackey and Jon Lester, and Shane Victorino slammed the door in Game 6.

76 — **ALDS**
Tampa Bay had been a thorn in Boston's side for a few years, but the Red Sox took care of their home field in dominating fashion, then eked out a victory in Game 4 to avoid a winner-take-all finale.

When it was over, left fielder **Jonny Gomes** donned his party gear.

Full circle

By helping Boston heal, Sox grew stronger

BY JOHN FARRELL

John Farrell absorbed many lessons from his tenure as Terry Francona's pitching coach.

Playing and managing in Boston, there's a history that we can't look past: The Hall of Fame players who have come through here, the championship teams that have played here before us, and the Red Sox, we feel, are very much a part of the fabric of this city, maybe more so than other places.

Along with that come the expectations, the inherent pressures, and this season's success began with the way that general manager Ben Cherington reshaped the roster – his ability to bring in those players who would embrace all that is Boston. That understanding and buying into a team concept by every player in our uniform, and an undeniable commitment and work ethic by our coaching staff, all these things allowed us to create an environment where we supported one another. We worked hard to prepare daily, and in particular for each series – which is probably the main reason why we didn't lose more than three games in a row at any one point during the year.

Starting with the first day of spring training, we wanted to make the game every single night the most important thing. By having one primary focus for all of us, I felt like that would guide our work, guide our thoughts and intentions, and potentially limit our distractions overall. So if the game every night is the most important thing, then we would do everything in our power to prepare for that.

Along the way, it was about how we played the game, a style of play, an aggressiveness, a relentlessness that to me is an attitude; it's a choice that you can consciously make. I think it's one thing that not only resonates with everyone in the clubhouse, but if we take that approach on the field, I think it begins to resonate with the fans, and they understand that we're giving our all every time we walk on the field.

Having been here under former manager Terry Francona and having seen first-hand what the atmosphere is, those experiences were invaluable this season. When issues arise internally in our clubhouse or with an individual, it's critical to handle them one-on-one behind closed doors, and not let any potential distractions grow into anything greater. We all recognize that this is a very difficult game to play, and the players need to know that there's a sanctuary in that clubhouse, so that when they go on the field they can be free of mind and compete to the best of their ability.

We felt like we had a roster full of good teammates, one that would unite and would play for one another. When the tragedy of April 15th hit, it was clear in everyone's mind – there was nothing organized, nothing structured, but everyone wanted to reach out in some way. Maybe we could bring some healing along the way, provide a distraction for them for two to three hours a night. There were other, more tangible things we could do – hospital visits, tickets given, contributions made – but we wanted to do whatever we could to help those in need, and we continue to remember those who have fallen victim.

We took that opportunity to help others, and along the way it helped to galvanize us. In a way, we became a vehicle for helping people to heal – people appreciated our grit, the way we played the game. Then it became a back-and-forth, the energy they provided, our players embraced it, they fed off it, and it was no more evident than in Game 6 of the World Series, how electric the atmosphere was at Fenway that night.

> IT'S ABOUT HOW WE PLAY THE GAME, A STYLE OF PLAY, A RELENTLESSNESS THAT TO ME IS AN ATTITUDE, IT'S A CHOICE THAT YOU CAN CONSCIOUSLY MAKE.

Having some idea of what it takes to thrive and succeed here from working under Tito, coming back and having an understanding of what to expect, we found players who had a very similar approach and a similar thought process to the game, and it worked. It came full circle.

To our fans, I just want to say that you're awesome – you were with us every step of the way. There might have been some bumps in those steps, but we feel you – we feel the energy that you create for us, and we are forever thankful. ∎

John Farrell is manager of the Boston Red Sox. This introduction was written with Ron Driscoll, Globe Correspondent.

Redeem team

Nothing fazed Boston's sons of destiny

BY CHRISTOPHER L. GASPER

The Next Great Red Sox team isn't an organizational catch phrase or a distant vision. It became a reality when the Red Sox won the 109th World Series. What was the Unthinkable Dream in February was as vivid and brilliant and real as the October foliage.

A year after finishing last in the American League East, the Red Sox are the last team standing. From pariahs to parade-planners, the Red Sox capped a remarkable turnaround with a 6-1 victory over the St. Louis Cardinals in Game 6 at Fenway Park to capture the franchise's third World Series title since 2004.

It couldn't have ended any other way. These retooled Red Sox were really, really good, with gamers and grinders, chemistry and camaraderie, run prevention and run generation. And they had destiny in their dugout. Certain seasons, certain teams just can't lose. The 2013 Red Sox were one of those teams.

Their fourth-choice closer, Koji Uehara, turned out to be the best closer in baseball. A pitcher they would have put in the Salvation Army donation bin if they could have, John Lackey, turned out to be their most consistent pitcher and won the clinching game of the World Series. The guy everyone in baseball said they overpaid for, Shane Victorino, won a Gold Glove, stopped switch-hitting, and came up with two huge bases-loaded postseason hits batting righthanded against righties.

This redoubtable team full of bushy faces and Boston Strong shoulders was a freight train on fate's tracks and nothing was going to derail them, certainly not the St. Louis Cardinals.

"People counted us out and we kept proving them wrong all year and now we're here with this trophy," said Red Sox ace Jon Lester.

It didn't all go right for the Red Sox this postseason, but it was close.

It started in the very first game, when Tampa Bay Rays right fielder Wil Myers inexplicably pulled off of a routine fly, paving the way for a five-run fourth inning and a 12-2 victory. It continued in the first game of the World Series, when the Cardinals played defense like the baseball was an invisible object.

On Oct. 30, fortune smiled on the Sons of Fenway once again. Victorino, who had been 0 for 10 in the series, hit a bases-loaded double in the third that gave the Sox a 3-0 lead.

With one out and Jacoby Ellsbury on first in the third, Cardinals manager Mike Matheny, perhaps by popular vote of the good folks of St. Louis, finally decided to stop pitching to David Ortiz and ordered an intentional walk.

But St. Louis starter Michael Wacha hit Johnny Gomes with two outs to load the bases. Victorino who delivered the Red Sox to the World Series with a seventh-inning grand slam in Game 6 of the American League Championship Series against the Detroit Tigers, drilled a three-run double high off the Green Monster.

He took third on the throw and pounded his chest with both hands while letting out a primal scream.

"Obviously, no one is 100 percent this time of year and for him

TO PARAPHRASE ORTIZ, THE WORLD SERIES MVP, THIS WAS JUST THE RED SOX BLEEPIN' SEASON.

Koji Uehara, who started the season as a setup man, was the MVP of the ALCS and closed out every playoff series, including the clincher vs. the Cards.

to go out there and compete and get that big knock, that's just our team," said Ellsbury. "That's just our team all year."

Victorino was a late scratch from Game 4 with lower back tightness. The man who replaced him, Gomes, ended up hitting a three-run homer that broke a 1-1 tie and powered the Sox to a 4-2 win, perhaps the single biggest hit of the series.

Victorino was out for Game 5 too, as manager John Farrell went with Gomes and Daniel Nava. The Sox usual No. 2 hitter, Farrell dropped him to sixth for Game 6, and he went 2 for 3 with four runs batted in and a pair of bases-loaded hits.

Fate.

If there was any doubt that the Red Sox were destined to win this World Series, it was put to rest with a three-run fourth.

Stephen Drew, who had last gotten a hit on Labor Day — OK, that's an exaggeration, he was 4 for 51 (.078) in the postseason — belted a first-pitch fastball into the Red Sox bullpen to lead off the fourth.

"He actually told me that he was going to hit a home run today," said first baseman Napoli, who took batting practice with Drew.

Of course he did. That's the way the 2013 Red Sox rolled.

With Ellsbury on third and two outs, Matheny intentionally walked Ortiz again. But he lifted Wacha, who had fanned cleanup batter Napoli twice. Napoli singled, of course, off Lance Lynn to drive in another run.

Victorino hit a bases-loaded single to left to score Ortiz and make it 6-0 and the barricades were going up outside of Fenway Park in anticipation of a flood of the Faithful.

Six runs was more than enough for Lackey, who could drink all the beer he wanted in the clubhouse after this one. Lackey left with two outs in the seventh and a 6-1 lead and tipping his cap to crowd.

Lackey had gone from an object of enmity among the Fenway Faithful to an object of idolatry.

"It gave me chills to hear the response that he deservedly received here," said Farrell. "It's almost fitting that he is the guy on the mound tonight to close it out. He mirrors the remake of this team and this organization."

The Red Sox joined the 1991 Minnesota Twins as the only teams to go from worst in their division to World Series winners. They also put 1918 to rest for good, becoming the first Red Sox team in 95 years to celebrate a World Series championship inside the baseball basilica in the Fens.

To paraphrase Ortiz, the World Series MVP, this was just the Red Sox bleepin' season. ∎

Christopher L. Gasper is a Globe columnist.

It all worked

With 2013 Red Sox, chemistry trumped talent

BY DAN SHAUGHNESSY

We are Boston. We love sports. We have brains and energy and tradition and history. Our young people carry their love of Boston teams when they move to other parts of the country and the world.

And those of us who have lived here for a while simply cannot believe what just unfolded with the Boston Red Sox in October of 2013.

The Duck Dynasty Sox got to ride the duck boats. They wheeled down Boylston Street past the sad spots where the bombs exploded in April. They did the right thing, just as they have done all season. They honored the dead and the maimed and the families of victims. And they were thankful for being allowed to help lift a region after the heinous events of Patriots Day.

Though it feels like this team invented Boston Strong, the Sox are only a major league baseball team, and it's neither fair nor respectful to overstate their role in our city's recovery from the tragedy. Still, manager John Farrell had it right when he said, "There's a civic responsibility that we have wearing this uniform, particularly here in Boston."

"We were playing for something more the rest of the year and we understood that," Dustin Pedroia said on ESPN.

Bottom line: After the death and disruption of mid-April, the 2013 Sox made most everyone in New England feel good again. The Sox were likable, and more important, they liked one another. A franchise famous for "25 guys, 25 cabs" became a magic bus of harmony, teamwork, and camaraderie. These highly paid, professional ballplayers actually enjoyed playing baseball and ignored the white noise that is so much a part of the Boston baseball experience.

In "Midnight Train to Georgia," Gladys Knight sings, "LA proved too much for the man." Boston baseball can be that way. Boston was too much for Adrian Gonzalez and Carl Crawford. Fortunately for Sox fans, Hub Hardball was a perfect fit for David Ross, Jonny Gomes, Mike Napoli, Stephen Drew, Ryan Dempster, Koji Uehara, and Shane Victorino.

They were the gang of seven free agents acquired by methodical, underrated general manager Ben Cherington after the train-wreck summer of 2012. Relieved of $261 million in future payroll obligations when the Dodgers took Carl and the Cooler, Cherington spent relatively short money on veteran "character" guys who had played in big markets and/or big games.

Everything worked. This Red Sox team was not as talented as the 2004 or 2007 teams. The Bearded Brotherhood is a classic example of the whole being greater than the sum of the parts.

In a way, the Sox were like a high school baseball team, snapping towels, giving wedgies, and assigning one another fuzzy nicknames. It would be easy to imagine the 2013 Sox holding team dinners at Mom Pedroia's house, wearing their uniforms to school on game days, and singing songs on the bus en route to rival schools. The 2013 Boston baseball season was played at the intersection of "Moneyball" and "Friday Night Lights."

This was the ultimate Team. It was worthy of your love and dedication from the jump. Unfortunately, after the Bobby V Show, folks were mad at the Sox and few fans got on board early. Many in the media doubted this team's ability to sustain its winning ways. We were wrong.

The 2013 Sox truly were a gift. ■

> **THE 2013 BOSTON BASEBALL SEASON WAS PLAYED AT THE INTERSECTION OF "MONEYBALL" AND "FRIDAY NIGHT LIGHTS."**

For the third time in 10 years, the duck boats rolled through the Back Bay with Red Sox aboard.

Dan Shaughnessy is a Globe columnist.

The Red Sox connected with their fans in a new way in 2013. There was beard bonding (**Will Middlebrooks** and **David Ross** were still playing up that note during the victory tour) and numerous nods to Boston Strong. "I'd just like to say thank you to the Red Sox for bringing all these people back to the streets for something so great to celebrate," said one parade-goer.

Game 6 winner **John Lackey** finally let down his hair and mingled with fans, and a particularly poignant moment came when **Jonny Gomes** and **Jarrod Saltalamacchia** joined the crowd in singing "God Bless America" at the Boston Marathon finish line.

Hundreds of thousands of fans converged on Boston for the parade, which rolled through the streets and into the Charles River on an unseasonably warm November day. Boston Police officer **Steve Horgan** reprised his victory pose, **David Ortiz** got behind the wheel of a duck boat, and **Jonny Gomes** held the trophy high, for all to see.

WORLD SERIES

This was getting to be a habit – the Red Sox have never faced any other World Series foe more than once, but this was their fourth clash with the Cardinals. As in the ALDS, Boston bolted to an easy (8-1) Game 1 victory. That is where the tracks diverged, as the Red Sox proceeded to lose two games in a row for the only time in the 2013 postseason, capped by the puzzling defeat by obstruction in Game 3. The gritty Sox went on to sweep the final three games, thanks to patchwork pitching in Game 4 and dominant starters Jon Lester and John Lackey in Games 5-6, not to mention the occasional timely hit, by Jonny Gomes (three-run homer in Game 4), David Ross (go-ahead RBI double in Game 5), and Shane Victorino (three-run double in Game 6, his second critical Game 6 blow of the postseason).

GAME 1 LIVIN' THE DREAM

In a repeat of their sloppy start to Game 1 of the 2004 World Series, the Cardinals made costly miscues that allowed the Red Sox to grab a quick 5-0 lead. Jon Lester scattered five hits and a walk to extend his career Series shutout streak to $13\frac{1}{3}$ innings, and David Ortiz homered and knocked in three runs.

CARDINALS | 000 000 001 173
RED SOX | 320 | 000 | 21 X | 881

The Series opened well for Boston, as **Mike Napoli** ripped a three-run double in the first and **David Ortiz** was greeted by **Dustin Pedroia** after his seventh-inning homer. **Jacoby Ellsbury** and **Shane Victorino** celebrated the 8-1 victory.

MAN OF THE GAME

DAVID ORTIZ

Big Papi was robbed of his second grand slam of this postseason by Carlos Beltran in the second inning, but he made sure of it in the seventh, sending the first pitch from Kevin Siegrist into the stands for a two-run homer. Ortiz also reached on an error and scored in the first inning.

"THIS TIME OF THE YEAR YOU REALLY HAVE TO THINK ABOUT WINNING EACH INNING.... YOU'VE GOT TO PUT A ZERO UP. GET THESE GUYS BACK IN THE DUGOUT AND GET THEM BACK IN THE BATTER'S BOX."

– JON LESTER
who pitched 7²/₃ shutout innings

Junichi Tazawa and **Ryan Dempster** (46) worked in relief, and his mates celebrated **David Ortiz's** run that made it 3-0 in the first inning, after the umpires overturned a call by Dana DeMuth at second base that had **John Farrell** livid. **Mike Napoli** and **Xander Bogaerts** reveled in the victory.

David Ortiz's two-run home run in the seventh inning was his 16th career postseason homer, moving him past Babe Ruth and into a tie for eighth all-time with Carlos Beltran of the Cardinals.

"I JUST EXPLAINED TO HIM THAT FIVE OF US WERE 100 PERCENT SURE. OUR JOB IS TO GET THE PLAY RIGHT." – UMPIRE JOHN HIRSCHBECK

1

KEY AT BAT

COLLECT CALL

Taking advantage of a controversial play at second base that loaded the bases one at-bat prior, **Mike Napoli** laced a three-run double to left-center field. The ball bounced to the wall, center fielder Shane Robinson took an awkward route to the carom and had a hard time picking it up, and the Red Sox were rolling.

1. 91 m.p.h. fastball

GAME2 LIVIN' THE DREAM

| CARDINALS | 000 | 100 | 300 | 471 |
| RED SOX | 000 | 002 | 000 | 242 |

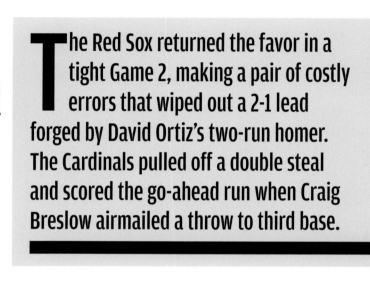

The Red Sox returned the favor in a tight Game 2, making a pair of costly errors that wiped out a 2-1 lead forged by David Ortiz's two-run homer. The Cardinals pulled off a double steal and scored the go-ahead run when Craig Breslow airmailed a throw to third base.

LIVIN' THE DREAM

A CELEBRATION OF THE WORLD CHAMPION 2013 BOSTON RED SOX | "I BELIEVE IT IS A MOMENTUM SPORT. I DON'T THINK THERE ARE STATISTICS TO

Jonny Gomes made a game effort on **Carlos Beltran's** line-drive single in the first; **Jacoby Ellsbury, Stephen Drew,** and the Sox lineup struggled until **David Ortiz's** two-run homer in the sixth; **Craig Breslow** (32) couldn't watch as the Cards celebrated taking the lead on his overthrow.

St. Louis baserunners Pete Kozma and Jon Jay executed a crucial double steal in the seventh inning off Sox reliever Craig Breslow. Cardinal baserunners had just 45 steals in the regular season, last in the National League.

Boston batters, including **Jonny Gomes, Jarrod Saltalamacchia,** and **Dustin Pedroia** (who had a loud foul) were frustrated by **Michael Wacha. John Lackey** was typically reluctant to leave the game.

"I'M SURE CRAIG WOULD LIKE TO HAVE THAT BALL BACK AND HOLD IT WITH THE CHANCE TO SHUT THE INNING DOWN RIGHT THERE"

– JOHN FARRELL
on Craig Breslow's wild throw to third base that allowed the go-ahead run to score

MAN OF THE GAME

MICHAEL WACHA

Wacha extended his rookie record scoreless string to 18²/₃ innings before he allowed a two-run homer to David Ortiz, and the 22-year-old got the victory when the Cards pushed across three runs in the seventh. He allowed just three hits in six innings, while walking four and striking out six.

Craig Breslow's throw sailed over **Stephen Drew,** allowing the go-ahead run to score, after the Cards had executed a double steal. **David Ortiz** greeted **Mariano Rivera,** who was honored by MLB before the game.

KEY AT BAT

WON WITH E'S

The Cardinals would have been content getting just the tying run on **Matt Carpenter's** sacrifice fly, but they also ended up plating the go-ahead run as the Red Sox committed a pair of errors. Jonny Gomes's momentum was going toward center field when he caught the ball, yanking his throw to the plate up the first-base line. Catcher Jarrod Saltalamacchia couldn't get a handle on the ball as pinch runner Pete Kozma scored. Pitcher Craig Breslow, backing up Saltalamacchia, overthrew Stephen Drew at third base, and Jon Jay was awarded home plate as the ball ended up in the crowd.

1. 88 m.p.h. fastball

GAME 3 LIVIN'THE DREAM

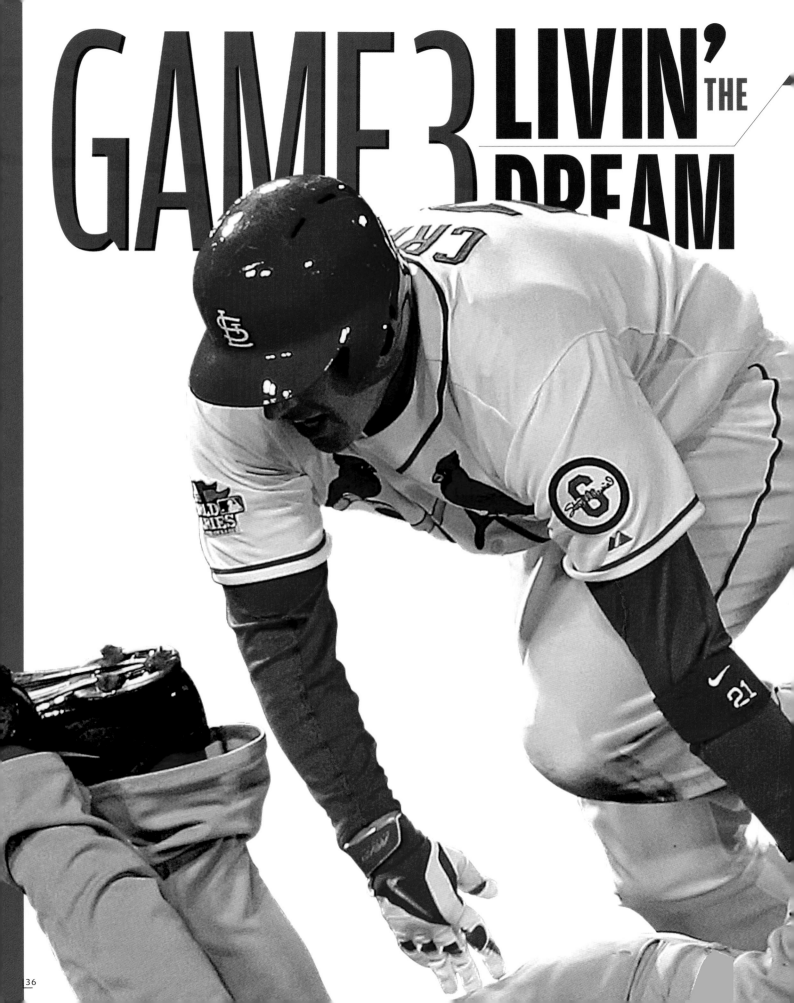

RED SOX		0 0 0	0 1 1	0 2 0	4 6 2
CARDINALS		2 0 0	0 0 0	2 0 1	5 12 0

St. Louis took a 2-1 Series advantage despite giving up a pair of two-run leads to the Red Sox. After Boston made it 4-4 in the eighth inning, Allen Craig touched up Sox closer Koji Uehara for a double, then lumbered home for the walk-off victory thanks to an obstruction call.

Jake Peavy worked out of a couple of jams, but left trailing, 2-0; **Xander Bogaerts** was safe at third in the fifth inning; **Shane Victorino** and **Jacoby Ellsbury** made outs, and Peavy conferred with **Jarrod Saltalamacchia.**

Major League Baseball Rule 7.06, in part: "If an infielder dives at a ground ball and the ball passes him and he continues to lie on the ground and delays the progress of the runner, he very likely has obstructed the runner."

"THIS WAS KIRK GIBSON-ESQUE. THAT'S WHAT THE POSTSEASON IS ABOUT AND THAT WAS A GUTSY PERFORMANCE." – MATT CARPENTER, CARDINALS' SECOND BASEMAN, ON ALLEN CRAIG

3

MAN OF THE GAME

ALLEN CRAIG

Before he became the obstructed baserunner, Craig rifled a double off Red Sox closer Koji Uehara in the ninth inning. He then hustled toward third base as the Red Sox nailed Yadier Molina at home, leading toward the errant throw by Jarrod Saltalamacchia. All this while playing on a badly injured foot.

Junichi Tazawa allowed a two-run double to **Matt Holliday** that scored **Carlos Beltran,** but he avoided further damage; **Shane Victorino** was hit by a pitch in Boston's eighth-inning rally; **Xander Bogaerts** awaited the late throw as **Kolten Wong** stole second in the eighth inning.

WHO WRIGGLED OUT OF A BASES-LOADED, NONE-OUT JAM IN THE FOURTH INNING, ALLOWED TWO RUNS ON SIX HITS AND LEFT WITH A 9.27 ERA IN FIVE POSTSEASON STARTS.

3

"I DON'T CARE WHAT ANYBODY SAYS. THAT'S NO WAY FOR A WORLD SERIES GAME TO END."

- DAVID ORTIZ

The Sox were in shock after **Saltalamacchia** tagged **Allen Craig** out, only to have the game end on an obstruction call against **Will Middlebrooks.** Earlier, **Dustin Pedroia** lent a hand to **David Ortiz** and **Stephen Drew** failed to connect.

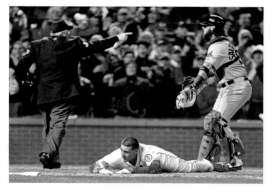

"I DON'T THINK WE'RE GOING TO GO HOME ANGRY. YOU'VE GOT TO HAVE THAT ABILITY TO WALK OUT OF THE CLUBHOUSE AND FORGET ABOUT IT." – JARROD SALTALAMACCHIA

3

KEY AT BAT

DOWN AND OUT

Jon Jay hit a hot shot grounder to second that a pulled-in Dustin Pedroia snagged. He fired to the plate, where Jarrod Saltalamacchia tagged Yadier Molina for the second out of the inning. Saltalamacchia then threw to third to try to get Allen Craig. The ball got by Will Middlebrooks, who was called for interference as Craig broke for home with the winning run.

1. 89 m.p.h. fastball
2. 81 m.p.h. splitter

The Game 3 victory gave the Cardinals a 13-1 record in their last 14 postseason games at Busch Stadium.

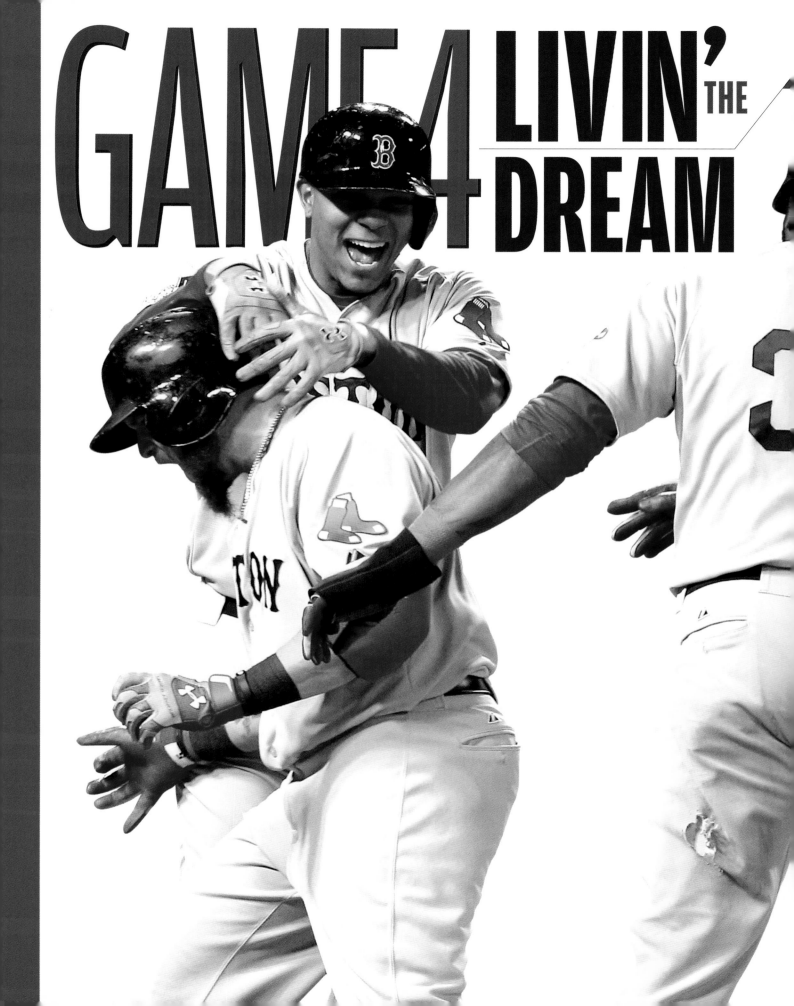

GAME 4

LIVIN' THE DREAM

RED SOX	000	013	000	462
CARDINALS	001	000	100	260

Clay Buchholz managed to give the Sox four innings of one-run pitching despite shoulder fatigue, and the Sox used erstwhile starters Felix Doubront and John Lackey to help get the game to closer Koji Uehara, who preserved the victory forged by a dramatic three-run homer by Jonny Gomes in the seventh.

Koji Uehara and **Mike Napoli** celebrated their game-ending pickoff of Cardinal pinch-runner **Kolten Wong**. **David Ortiz** kept himself in the game and got the Red Sox on the board in the fifth inning. **Xander Bogaerts** was solid at third base.

Felix Doubront earned the victory in relief, going 2²/₃ innings while allowing one run on one hit, striking out three and walking none. Doubront also pitched two scoreless innings in Game 3.

THE RED SOX IMPROVED TO 7-1 IN THE POSTSEASON WHEN THEY HIT A HOME RUN. THE ONLY LOSS WAS IN GAME 2 OF THE WORLD SERIES, WHEN THEY FELL, 4-2, DESPITE A DAVID ORTIZ HOMER.

4

MAN OF THE GAME

JONNY GOMES

Shortly after David Ortiz called his troops over for a dugout meeting, Gomes cracked the three-run homer that would seal Game 4 and put frustrating Game 3 squarely in the rear-view mirror. "When I'm in the lineup, I'm going to be swinging," said Gomes, who was 1 for his previous 18 going into the at-bat.

David Ortiz was safe at home in the fifth, **Clay Buchholz** gave the Sox four innings on a tired arm, and outfielders **Jonny Gomes, Jacoby Ellsbury,** and **Daniel Nava** celebrated the victory, which was sealed by **Mike Napoli's** tag on the Cards' **Kolten Wong. Felix Doubront** was solid in relief. Before Gomes struck in the seventh, Pedroia fanned in the fourth.

"WE HAVE A REAL RESILIENT TEAM. WE PLAY FOR EACH OTHER AND CARE FOR EACH OTHER. ... WE HAVE GUYS OUT THERE LIKE JONNY WHO WOULD RUN THROUGH A WALL FOR ANYBODY ON THIS TEAM."

– DAVID ROSS
on Game 4 hero Jonny Gomes

"I WAS JUST RELAXED AND DOING MY JOB. WHEN I GOT THE OPPORTUNITY I WAS SO FOCUSED IN. ... JUST FOCUSING ON GETTING OUTS." – FELIX DOUBRONT

4

KEY AT BAT

SUDDENLY TANGIBLE

An inning after **Jonny Gomes** drew a 10-pitch walk off Cardinals starter Lance Lynn, Boston's left fielder was due up again with runners on first and second and two out. Lynn was lifted in favor of righthander Seth Maness, who ran the count to 2-2 on four straight sinkers. Gomes, whom manager John Farrell has praised this postseason for his intangibles, crushed the fifth sinker into the seats in left field, giving the Red Sox a 4-1 lead.

1. 90 m.p.h. sinker
2. 90 m.p.h. sinker
3. 89 m.p.h. sinker
4. 90 m.p.h. sinker
5. 90 m.p.h. sinker

John Lackey contributed an inning of relief after Gomes celebrated his long ball. **Matt Carpenter** (43) logged the Cards' only run in the third, and **Craig Breslow** left the mound after a disappointing outing.

NO PREVIOUS WORLD SERIES GAME HAD ENDED WITH A BASERUNNER GETTING PICKED OFF.

4

Jonny Gomes was 0 for 9 with a walk in the World Series before he clubbed the three-run homer that would prove the game-winner. The Red Sox improved to 8-1 in the postseason in games in which Gomes started in left field.

GAME 5 LIVIN' THE DREAM

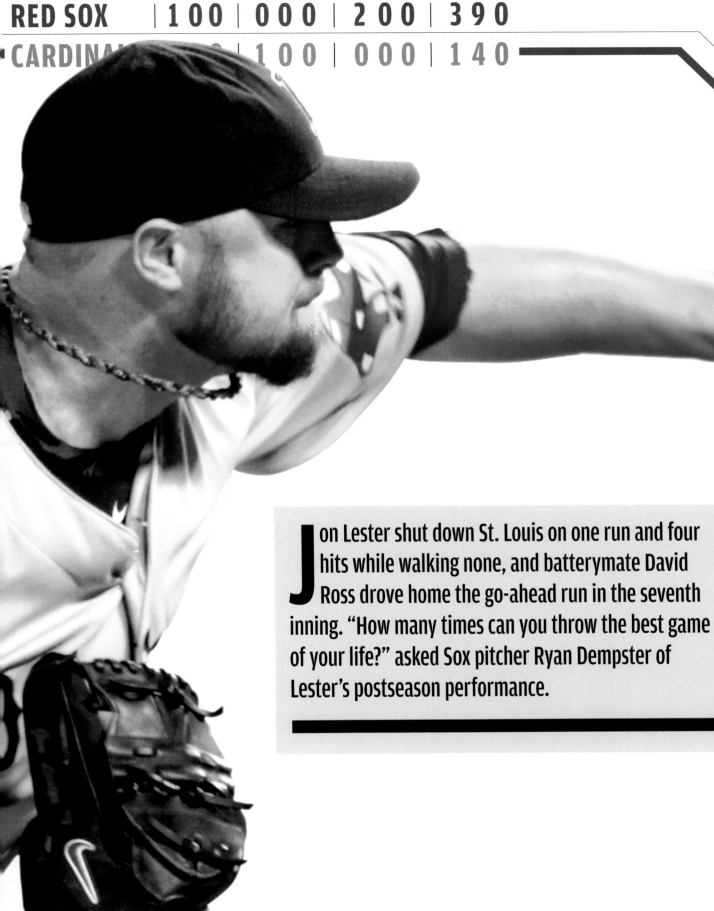

RED SOX | 1 0 0 | 0 0 0 | 2 0 0 | 3 9 0

CARDINALS | | 1 0 0 | 0 0 0 | 1 4 0

Jon Lester shut down St. Louis on one run and four hits while walking none, and batterymate David Ross drove home the go-ahead run in the seventh inning. "How many times can you throw the best game of your life?" asked Sox pitcher Ryan Dempster of Lester's postseason performance.

David Ross congratulated **Jon Lester** as Lester exits in the seventh inning. Red Sox hitters such as **Jacoby Ellsbury** (center), Ross and Lester (attempting a bunt) were stymied, but **David Ortiz** had three hits.

Jon Lester improved to 3-0 in three career World Series starts. In the 2013 postseason, he went 4-1 over 34^2/$_3$ innings, allowing 25 hits and fanning 29 with a 1.56 ERA.

MAN OF THE GAME

JON LESTER

The Red Sox ace outdueled Adam Wainwright for the second time in the Series, giving up one run on four hits with seven strikeouts. In 21 innings of World Series pitching, his numbers are staggering: one run allowed on 12 hits, with 18 strikeouts, four walks and a 0.43 ERA.

David Ross was out at home trying to score the fourth run, but Red Sox infielders **Stephen Drew** and **Dustin Pedroia** made the key plays and **Koji Uehara** got the final four outs to send the Sox back to Boston happy. **David Ortiz** (right) was a familiar presence on the basepaths with three hits, including a double.

"I HAD TO DO SOMETHING. JUST SOMETHING LITTLE TO HELP MOVE THE LINE."

– STEPHEN DREW

who reached on a walk and scored in the seventh-inning rally, after going 1 for 14 to that point in the World Series.

AVID ORTIZ'S RBI DOUBLE IN THE FIRST INNING GAVE HIM 14 IN WORLD SERIES PLAY, TYING HIM WITH DWIGHT EVANS FOR THE TEAM RECORD AND GIVING HIM THE MOST OF ANY ACTIVE PLAYER.

5

KEY AT BAT

DOUBLE HIS PLEASURE

Another bearded wonder, **David Ross**, came through in the clutch for the Red Sox. The veteran catcher, more known for his defense than his bat, came up against Cardinals ace Adam Wainwright with runners on first and second and one out in the seventh. Facing a 1-2 count, Ross laced a curveball down the left-field line and the ball bounced into the seats for a ground-rule double. Xander Bogaerts scored on the hit, giving Boston a 2-1 lead.

1. 88 m.p.h. cutter
2. 91 m.p.h. fastball
3. 88 m.p.h. cutter

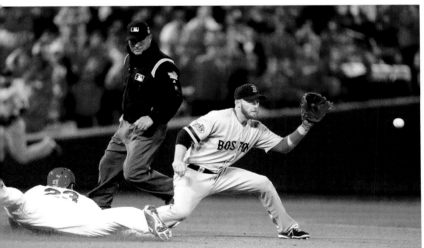

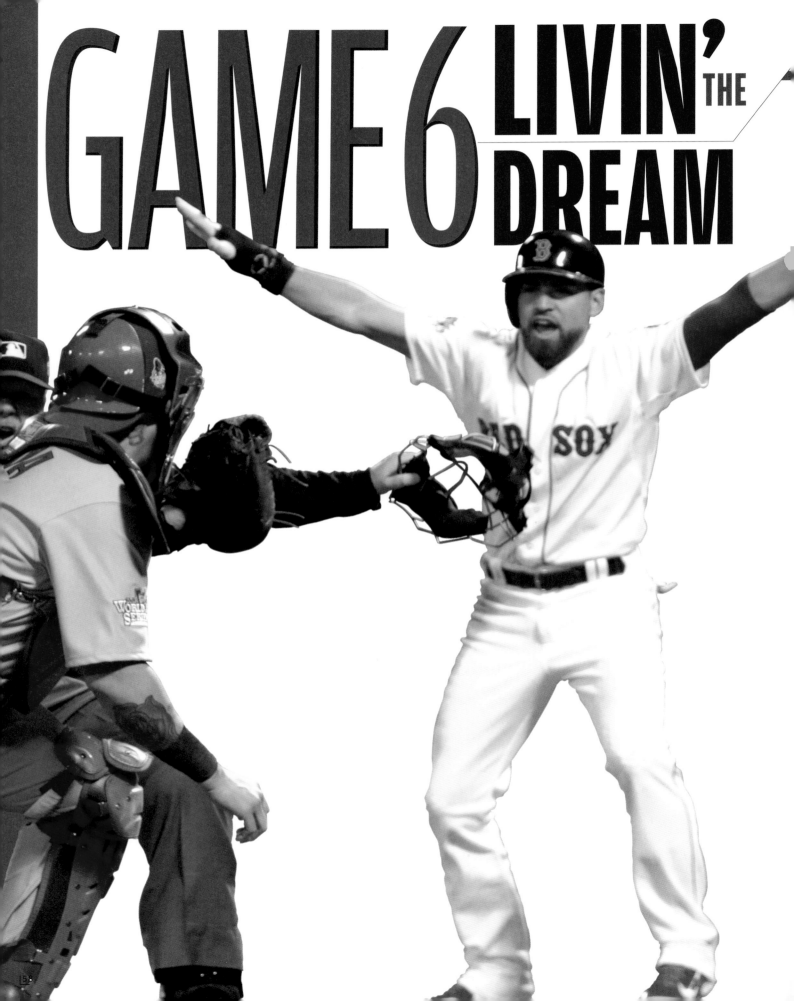

GAME 6 LIVIN' THE DREAM

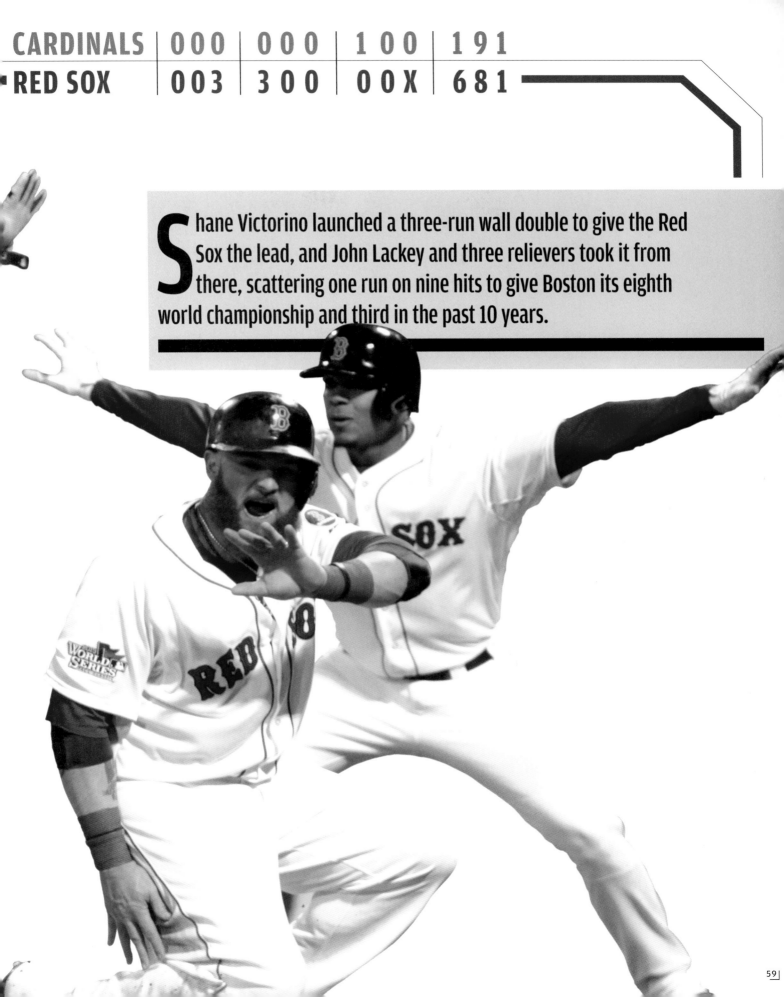

CARDINALS	000	000	100	191
RED SOX	003	300	00X	681

Shane Victorino launched a three-run wall double to give the Red Sox the lead, and John Lackey and three relievers took it from there, scattering one run on nine hits to give Boston its eighth world championship and third in the past 10 years.

It's unanimous, **Jonny Gomes** is safe at home on **Shane Victorino's** three-run double (previous page), staking **John Lackey** to an early lead. Lackey coaxed **John Farrell** to keep him in, and **Jacoby Ellsbury** wriggled out of a Cardinal pickoff try. **Stephen Drew** came through with a solo homer in the fourth inning.

THE RED SOX WON THEIR EIGHTH WORLD SERIES, BREAKING A TIE WITH THE GIANTS AND MOVING INTO FOURTH PLACE ALL-TIME, BEHIND THE YANKEES (27), CARDINALS (11), AND A'S (9).

6

MAN OF THE GAME

JOHN LACKEY

Lackey's rebound from missing the entire 2012 season due to Tommy John surgery was capped by his postseason efforts, which included an inning of crucial relief in Game 4 and the clinching Game 6 victory. He scattered nine hits and one walk, giving up just one run in $6\frac{2}{3}$ innings.

Koji Uehara, who was on the mound for the final out of each of the three playoff series in 2013, had seven postseason saves, matching the all-time record for a single postseason. Four other pitchers have done it, most recently the Phillies' Brad Lidge in 2008.

Shane Victorino hit the wall, **Jonny Gomes** got hit, and **Mike Napoli** hit the ground running after an RBI single.

"NO DISRESPECT TO ANYBODY, THE BEATING OF THE CHEST – IT'S JUST EXCITEMENT. GETTING TO THIRD BASE, SHOWING THE EMOTION THAT I DID – THAT HAPPINESS, THAT JOYFULNESS, THE LOUDNESS OF FENWAY ON ITS FEET."

– SHANE VICTORINO
on his reaction to his three-run double

"ONCE THE GAME IS TAKEN AWAY FROM YOU BECAUSE OF AN INJURY, YOU BEGIN TO APPRECIATE IT MUCH MORE WHEN YOU COME BACK." – JOHN FARRELL

6

KEY AT BAT

HAWAIIAN, THREE-O

Shane Victorino's ALCS grand slam was on the minds of fans when he stepped to the plate with the bases loaded and two out in the bottom of the third inning. While he fell a bit shy of another home run, his three-run, wall-ball double off Michael Wacha started the party at Fenway, putting the Sox up, 3-0, en route to a World Series-clinching victory.

1. 74 m.p.h. curveball
2. 92 m.p.h. fastball
3. 93 m.p.h. fastball
4. 93 m.p.h. fastball

Dustin Pedroia and **John Farrell** basked in the victory after players swarmed the field to celebrate the final strikeout by **Koji Uehara**.

The Red Sox are the second team to win a World Series one year after finishing in last place in its division. The Minnesota Twins accomplished the feat in 1991. The Red Sox also became just the fourth team since 1995 – when the Division Series was added – to win the Series after earning the best record in MLB.

"THIS TOWN, WE STRUGGLED EARLY THIS YEAR WITH THE SITUATION ALL OF US WENT THROUGH. WE KEPT OURSELVES TOGETHER. HERE WE ARE. ENJOY YOUR TIME." – DAVID ORTIZ

6

ALCS LIVIN' THE DREAM

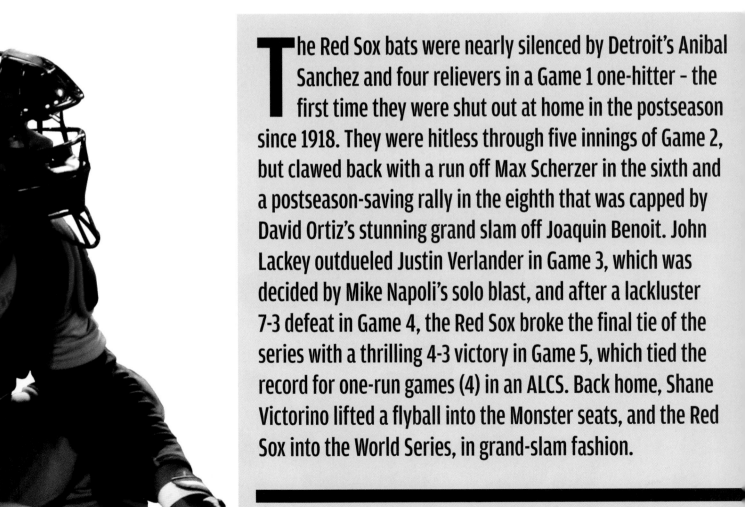

The Red Sox bats were nearly silenced by Detroit's Anibal Sanchez and four relievers in a Game 1 one-hitter – the first time they were shut out at home in the postseason since 1918. They were hitless through five innings of Game 2, but clawed back with a run off Max Scherzer in the sixth and a postseason-saving rally in the eighth that was capped by David Ortiz's stunning grand slam off Joaquin Benoit. John Lackey outdueled Justin Verlander in Game 3, which was decided by Mike Napoli's solo blast, and after a lackluster 7-3 defeat in Game 4, the Red Sox broke the final tie of the series with a thrilling 4-3 victory in Game 5, which tied the record for one-run games (4) in an ALCS. Back home, Shane Victorino lifted a flyball into the Monster seats, and the Red Sox into the World Series, in grand-slam fashion.

The ALCS got off to a rocky start for Boston; **Quintin Berry** (50) stole second in the last of the ninth in Game 1, but the Sox were one-hit in a 1-0 defeat as **Jon Lester** took the loss. **Dustin Pedroia** and David Ortiz struck out in Game 2 before Ortiz provided the series-saving homer; **Jarrod Saltalamacchia** drove in the winning run in Game 2; **Jake Peavy** (44) struggled in Game 4.

"BEFORE THE SERIES EVEN STARTED, IT WAS 'VERLANDER, VERLANDER, VERLANDER' IN GAME 3. YOU ABSOLUTELY TIP YOUR HAT TO VERLANDER. HE PITCHED A HECK OF A GAME, BUT I THINK WE CAN TALK ABOUT JOHN LACKEY A LITTLE BIT, TOO."

– JONNY GOMES
Red Sox left fielder

Mike Napoli homered to make a winner of **John Lackey** in Game 3; **Koji Uehara** saved that victory, and two others; **Miguel Cabrera** struck out against **Junichi Tazawa** for a key eighth-inning out in Game 3; **Dustin Pedroia** turned a Game 5 double play; Boston Police officer **Steve Horgan** signaled victory as **Torii Hunter** tumbled in vain on Ortiz's Game 2 grand slam.

The Red Sox offense produced one hit in the first 14 innings of the ALCS and trailed 5-1 in Game 2 before David Ortiz clocked a game-tying grand slam with two outs in the bottom of the eighth against Detroit closer Joaquin Benoit.

Mike Napoli connected on his second homer of the series in Game 5; **Xander Bogaerts** doubled during a second-inning rally in Game 5; **Dustin Pedroia** belted a single in Game 6; **Mike Carp** saluted the fans with some post-victory bubbly.

Koji Uehara, initially signed to fill a setup role for the Red Sox, picked up a win and three saves to earn MVP honors in the ALCS. He struck out eight and walked none over six innings of work, allowing just four hits.

BEFORE HE HIT A GRAND SLAM IN THE SEVENTH INNING OF GAME 6 OF THE ALCS. IT WAS HIS SECOND CAREER GRAND SLAM IN POSTSEASON PLAY, TYING JIM THOME FOR THE ALL-TIME RECORD.

73

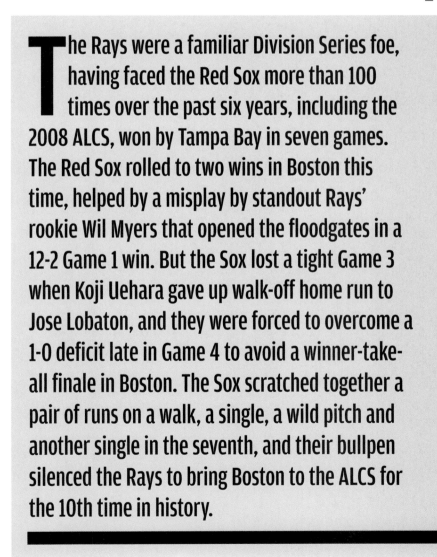

ALDS LIVIN' THE DREAM

The Rays were a familiar Division Series foe, having faced the Red Sox more than 100 times over the past six years, including the 2008 ALCS, won by Tampa Bay in seven games. The Red Sox rolled to two wins in Boston this time, helped by a misplay by standout Rays' rookie Wil Myers that opened the floodgates in a 12-2 Game 1 win. But the Sox lost a tight Game 3 when Koji Uehara gave up walk-off home run to Jose Lobaton, and they were forced to overcome a 1-0 deficit late in Game 4 to avoid a winner-take-all finale in Boston. The Sox scratched together a pair of runs on a walk, a single, a wild pitch and another single in the seventh, and their bullpen silenced the Rays to bring Boston to the ALCS for the 10th time in history.

Jacoby Ellsbury scored the first run of Game 3, and **Shane Victorino** legged out an infield hit that scored Ellsbury with the winning run in Game 4. **David Ortiz** homered twice off **David Price** in Game 2; **John Lackey** won Game 2 for Boston, which featured a steal by Ellsbury; Boston's outfielders celebrated the Game 1 win.

David Ortiz hit two homers off David Price in Game 2 of the series, a 7-4 Boston win. It was his first two-homer game in the postseason amd the first for the Red Sox since Dustin Pedroia hit two in Game 2 of the 2008 ALCS against Tampa Bay.

Jonny Gomes charged home in the fifth inning of Game 1; **Clay Buchholz** delivered a Game 3 pitch; **Jacoby Ellsbury** capitalized on a throwing error to score in Game 3; the Sox celebrated their series-clinching Game 4 victory.

"IT WAS A HARD THING TO SWALLOW, SINCE THE TEAM HAD JUST COME BACK. I WANTED TO GIVE THEM AN OPPORTUNITY TO GET BACK ON THE FIELD."

– KOJI UEHARA
after surrendering a walkoff homer to Jose Lobaton in Game 3

2012 VS. 2013

69-93

Were **53-51** at the end of July, but went **16-42** in the final two months of the season to finish last in AL East. Lost 12 of final 13 games.

SCORED 734 RUNS, ALLOWED 806 RUNS. (MINUS 72)
Went 5-13 vs. Yankees, scoring 70 runs and allowing 116

DUSTIN PEDROIA
"**I don't really understand what Bobby's trying to do.** Maybe that works in Japan. But that's really not the way we go about our stuff here. I'm sure he'll figure that out soon." – on Valentine questioning Kevin Youkilis's work ethic in April

JON LESTER
9-14 record, **4.82** ERA
110 earned runs allowed in **205.1** innings

GAMES PLAYED
David Ortiz: **90**
Jacoby Ellsbury: **74**

BEN CHERINGTON ON 2012
"**Last year was a forearm shiver to the face.** There was no ignoring that something needed to change, that we needed to do a better job. There was no explaining it away."

97-65

Began season **12-4,** and held first place for all but 19 days of season. Went **17-4** from Aug. 24 to Sept. 15, going from a first-place tie to a 9½-game lead.

SCORED 853 RUNS, ALLOWED 656 RUNS. (PLUS 197)
Went 13-6 vs. Yankees, scoring 120 runs and allowing 85

DUSTIN PEDROIA
"**Nobody cares about what they do personally. It's about the team.** Nobody remembers what David [Ortiz] hit in 2007 when we won the World Series. They just know we won the World Series."

JON LESTER
15-8 record, **3.75** ERA
89 earned runs allowed in **213.1** innings

GAMES PLAYED
David Ortiz: **137**
Jacoby Ellsbury: **134**

BEN CHERINGTON ON 2013
"**We had a group of guys returning who were so motivated** and weren't happy with the way things went. They wanted to prove that's not who they were. We had a group that completely got it."

WELCOME TO
FENWAY PARK
AMERICA'S MOST BELOVED BALLPARK

HOME OF THE BOSTON RED SOX

MITSUBISHI ELECTRIC

nk of America

LCOME
TO
AY PARK

5:45

AMERICA'S
MOST BELOVED
BALLPARK

ALEX AND ANI

GIANT
GLASS

Mercedes-Benz

NESN.COM

420

jetBlue

GRANITE CITY
ELECTRIC SUPPLY

Between 1997-2002, he split playing time between the Minnesota Twins and their minor-league affiliate, the New Britain (Conn.) Rock Cats.

HR: 30, RBI: 103, BA: .309, 2Bs: 38 / 7th 30-HR, 100-RBI year tied Williams.

GOMES: A soldier at the Natick, Mass., U.S. Army Research Institute of Environmental Medicine donated his advanced combat helmet from his tour of Iraq to Gomes.

HR: 13, RBI: 52, BA: .247, 2Bs: 17 / The Sox are Gomes' fifth team in six seasons

LESTER

He and his wife Farrah established NVRQT, short for "Never Quit," in 2011 to support the Pediatric Cancer Research Foundation.

W-L: 15-8, ERA: 3.75, GS: 33, Inn. 213.1 / Won his 100th game in AL East clincher.

FARRELL: Grew up on the Jersey Shore, one of six children of a lobsterman. Played most of his career with the Cleveland Indians.

W-L: 251-235; Age: 51; Managed: Tor., Bos.
Went 36-46 as MLB pitcher in 8 seasons.

SALTALAMACCHIA: At 14 characters, the West Palm Beach, Fla., native's last name is the longest in MLB history.

HR: 14, RBI: 65, BA: .273, 2Bs: 40
Had career batting highs in all but HRs, 3Bs.

Over past three seasons encompassing more than 1,200 at-bats, has a higher average vs. righties (.271) than lefties (.263).

HR: 23, RBI: 92, BA: .259, 2Bs: 38 Has at least 20 HRs in 6 straight seasons.

In the seven years before he signed with Boston, Lackey ranked in the top five among American League starters in victories, strikeouts, shutouts, and starts.

W-L: 10-13, ERA: 3.52, GS: 29, Inn. 189.1
7th in AL in strikeout/walk ratio (4.03).

PEDROIA

Was one of five finalists for college baseball's Golden Spikes Award while playing at Arizona State in 2004.... Fascinated with Bigfoot (a "Sasquatch Crossing" sign serves as his Twitter avatar).

HR: 9, RBI: 84, BA: .301, 2Bs: 42
2nd in AL in singles, T-2 in hits, T-3 in 2Bs.

BUCHHOLZ: In March 2011, he released his own wine label under the Longball Cellars brand, with sale proceeds going to the Jimmy Fund.

W-L: 12-1, ERA: 1.74, GS: 16, Inn. 108.1
Has a 58-33 career record over 7 seasons.

VICTORINO: Son of a Maui County councilman, he is an Eagle Scout. He had a brief acting role in an episode of "Hawaii Five-O," playing a character called Shaun.

HR: 15, RBI: 61, BA: .294, SB: 21/24
Tied for AL lead with 9 assists in RF.

ELLSBUR

Jacoby began his Red Sox career with the Lowell Spinners of New York-Penn League. Among his teammates were pitcher Clay Buchholz and infielder Jed Lowrie.

HR: 9, RBI: 53, BA: .298, SB: 52/56
Best rate (93%) for 50-steal man since 1922.

UEHARA: Enters the game at Fenway Park to a Norwegian techno pop song: Darude's "Sandstorm."

W-L: 4-1, ERA: 1.09 App.: 71, Saves: 21 / Allowed just 33 hits and 9 BBs in 74.1 innings.

It was a festive atmosphere during Game 6 of the World Series at Fenway, where a foul ball was highly prized. Beards and coats helped keep the faithful - and the "Teammates" - warm and stylish. Later, fans celebrated the clincher all over town, including at Mass. Ave. and Boylston Street.

Frenzied fandom reigned outside Fenway Park before and during the World Series, which ended with Boston's third title in a decade.

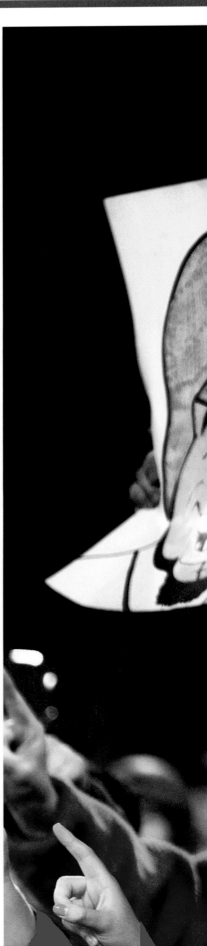

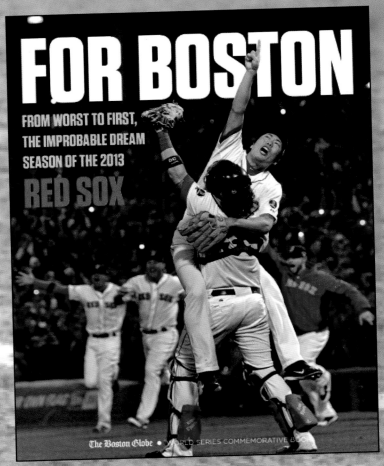